A Soul's Musings

by Sonia J Grover

BIBLIOTHECA AETERNA

First edition published in Great Britain by

Bibliotheca Aeterna in 2013

*

ISBN 978-0-9575947-8-4

Soul:

Depth, Individual, Gospel, Spirit, Person

Musings:

Thoughtful, Thinking, Contemplating, Reflective

Introduction

I was sitting in a café in Norway on the 28th December 2012 and it came to me to write a little book of musings, of thoughts, sayings and poems that I had been inspired to write over the years.

It has been an amazing experience, when I would ask myself about something that was happening to me, I started to have words appear in my head. So I started to write down what I was getting and it somehow seemed to be guidance from outside of myself, some people call this channelling.

It is my wish, that even if you find one word of this book makes you ponder, makes you question, then I am wealthy indeed, with gratitude, with love.

Blessings to you all.

Reality

Reality only exists once a person has perceived it and in that perception their reality is established, is made real.

Therefore nothing is real, there is no reality, it is simply the perception we give it.

Unconditional Love

Unconditional love is what they say

That we are all here to learn

As we live each day

So what does this mean as I wait in line

With those behind and in front of me

Getting agitated by the wait

Or the couple in front of me at the checkout

Making me late

Or the driver cutting in and out of the lane

Or a million other things that happen each day

That just seem to be a pain

Well what I learnt along my way

Is to choose what I think what I do and what I say

To realise in some strange and mystical way

That what I give out comes back to me, a thousand fold

No matter how hard I pray

It's as simple as the sunshine and the rain

What I give out, if it's not love, will return to me as pain

This journey through life has made me understand

That unconditional love is always and only

The real choice at hand

This Land of Mine

This land of mine was given to all

With great beauty to behold

From Mother Earth and Father Sky

The rising Moon and the setting Sun,

For all us creatures to live in

To grow and sow and manifest our dreams

This land of mine, was so serene

Yet full of so many wondrous sights to breathe

For not just my sight will see

But all my senses are activated in harmony

This land of mine, we thought we owned

And thought we knew how to prosper and to grow

And in our ignorance and wonton, it came to pass

The land no more filled with grass

No more the trees grew tall and stout

No more the birds and animals would sing and shout

This land of mine

This land of mine has taught me much

(If only I had listened before)

That to nurture, to sow and grow

In these times especially

Needs love like never before

And so I give honour and tribute

To my faithful friend who knew

That love and respect are the only traits that are true

I pay homage to this land of mine

How to Be

As I look into my soul

What is it I may see

Absolute perfection, no more no less, just me

So why then when I live

In my human form each day

Why do I think and act and criticise

With many words I say

As I come to understand that

Thoughts and words and deeds create

That I am manifesting all this anguish and hate

No more will this feed and nourish me

No more will this sustain life as it was meant to be

A change, a sea of wind is needed

By each and everyone

To manifest the perfection that

Has been, will be and is yet to come

How you may ask can this be done

Quite simply I say by remembering we are all one

One mind, one body, one form

Separated into millions of pieces

To allow growth and evolvement

Of perfection to be the norm

However, we need to allow this into our consciousness

To bring this into reality,

So we truly understand

What it means how to be

Who are You?

High above the clouds again in this tranquil ebb and flow

Feeling like a feather floating to wherever they go

Where everything is still, where the birds do not shrill

Up here in the clouds

Looking down on life as lands pass me by

Never really having to consider even why

In the clouds up high, where nothing really is

Time stands still

And the only sound you feel is the beating of your heart

This is where it's real, where you can just be

And through the stillness comes complete clarity

A complete and utter knowing of what it's all about

The how, the what, the where, the when

Illuminating my being

This is when you really know, you really understand

The only point in being here is to love

Every living being as unconditionally as you can

So who are you, my love, that I meet again

Now I am flying high, I know, as I meet you in these clouds

As sorrow, jealousy, rage and anger dissolve

Like specs of sand

For who you are, is a part of me

Now and forever, always will be

Stonehenge

❀

Having visited Stonehenge many times I asked what the stones were there for, what purpose they have to us all and this is what I was given.

❀

The stones are tablets or givers, for they give from the earth, to the people of the earth. The energy will affect all, some universally, some less so, when the storms of darkness ring down and so the purification process begins ever more so and as always. The symbology of the stones transcends time and space, providing a haven of transmission and transgression. The stones were placed mythically, then translucently, then became as you see now. As you know with the aid of transfiguration, they were placed using symbolic sacred geometry. Each line, each angle, each position in the ground was carefully placed and corresponds with its exact polarity. But this polarity is not opposite, as you would know it, and in a way at angles that you are only just beginning to understand.

This is how the great vortices are linked, of course, over ground, but more strongly linking in through Mother Earth, feeding her and feeding from her. So the reason was to feed the earth, to nourish her and all the people of the earth, now and forever more.

The energies from above, feed through the hills in a sacred geometric pattern, to assist in the feeding and cleansing process – these portals exist as mirrors in other universes, so now no actual visitation is required – although this does still happen, providing on some occasions energy signs, that you know as crop circles.

A Message for the Mountain People

❖

This was information I was given after a friend told me about a project she was working on, in a remote South American country. She was working with the local people to help re plant the land after some of the local land owners had sold the land to large timber companies and the land was laid bare. The local people asked if they could put it into their local newsletter and this was read at the next local ceremony/gathering of all the peoples.
The poem entitled "This land of Mine" was also given at the same time for these people. However I feel that this could apply to any land, any people.

❖

Oh Dear ones, my beloved mountain people

My people of the earth and the skies

It is once again I come to you

From your ancestors, the ancient ones

To rejoice with you and give thanks under the stars

On the fifth moon of the twilight zone

I am honoured and humbled by your gracious work,

Time is off the now

The sacred ones are passing their old teachings

Back to you

You must dance your merry dance

Sing the mountainous song

And breathe the mountainous air

Draw your sacred symbols in and with the land

Watch the Puma as he strolls

And the moon as it sleeps

And here lies the answers you search

Each star in a triangle past a square, by the stream

This is where you plant,

The number 13 as always will be

Part of your sacred planting

Roots, Herb, Heather and Mice

Are needed to sustain the life,

Channels for irrigation

Set diametrically and with symbolawareness

In line with the sun and the moon at angles of 13%

Watch the Puma walk

Smell the mountain heather bush

And this is where you plant,

Roots, Herbs Heather, Roots, Herbs, Heather

So farewell my children of the mountains

Long may you dwell

Truth

❊

The following texts were given to me over a period of time, after I asked the meaning for humans on these subjects.

❊

This is about your personal truths, not the truths of others. It is about being open and opening up to your own soul's truth. It is about letting go of old paradigms, old ways of thinking and being that no longer serve you. This may take many forms, as it makes you aware that this energy, is ready to be released, to be transmuted. It may take the form of physical pains, often in areas of the body where energy has been stuck before. It may take the form of emotions, where you may feel very ungrounded and "not yourself". It may take the form of thoughts, where you may experience a number of negative thought pattern types such as anger. Be calm, my children of God, for all is as it is meant to be. These changes are positive and can just be considered akin to growing pains, for make no mistake my beloved ones, growth is what is happening: Personal growth, family growth, community growth, country growth, world growth and universal growth. Our beloved Mother Earth is growing and cleansing. This is important to understand — which you already know — we are all one. We are all unique individuals who are part of the one. Others may help you discover your personal truth, but remember, it is your truth, not theirs, for it is your journey, your creation and your consciousness.

Transformation

This process of evolvement is always a choice: A choice of joy, sadness, love, jealousy, anger, or whichever emotion you have chosen to experience. Now is the time to remember that when you are experiencing these feelings, these thoughts, these emotions you always have a choice; a choice to experience whatever you wish. How may this be done – you may ask? Quite simply, I say, by choosing the emotion or feeling and welcoming it. It has surfaced for a reason, a reason of understanding. It matters not what level of understating you may have, this level is perfect for you at this time. Simply welcome the feeling or emotion.

Transmutation

To transmute is simply to change from one form of energy to another. So, if you choose to experience grief, simply welcome grief, feel grief, understand the grief and then let it go. Consciously choose to change the grief to feelings of happiness. You can all do this, my children, for you are all beings, all small parts of God. This is transmutation, like Alchemy, a changing of the energy at an atomic level. You are all healers and this you have seen: how physical pains and negative emotions are transformed into feelings of peace and love. Use this as a guide for yourself, use your imagination to transmute, ask the beings of light for help and it will be done.

Life is a journey, a journey to discover love.

No more, no less.

Peace, love and joy to you all.

Namaste.

❀

Namaste is the Indian (or Hindu) way of greeting each other meaning "I bow to you".

❀

Limitation

Limitation is a word that exists everywhere, but is far too prominent, my children, in your world here on earth. It was created to help with balance and for you to know your own limits in any given situation.

It was never meant to be used by you or your brethren to lessen or diminish your grandness or your vibration of love and light.

And so it came to pass that limitation became a part of your world: limitation of the self, limitation of your uniqueness, limitation of imagination, limitation of creation itself.

This was never meant to be but it is here, it is now a part and parcel of each person's psyche. Limitation is now ingrained in every cell of your being. It is how you have learned over eons of being how to live.

But do not fear or worry my children for as one of your teachers would say: "The time is now".

It is a very simple process to change or transmute: "The Power of Now". Simply use your imagination to create in your mind that which you wish. It is a process that you have done all your life, through play, through contemplation. For this visualisation, my children, is your tool for the process of evolution, to create your own reality – a reality without limitation.

So when you recognise your thoughts, words, actions and deeds full of limitation, choose to dissolve this limitation with light.
My dear ones, you may not know what to create or visualise. It does not matter, simply create light and this

will enlighten the visualisation. And ask it to bring that, which is for your highest good and the highest good of all humanity.

As your vibration, consciousness and awareness is opened and raised, so your ability to create with light increases. When you are ready, every level of limitation will dissolve. But do not worry, my children of God, for you will only create that which you are able to perceive and live.

It is grand indeed in a way that you will come to know. As your feelings of love are felt more deeply, more frequently, your smile will radiate outward more and more to enhance every living and non-living particle of existence.

What is it All About?

So it came to pass on this day many eons ago that these energies came before, to help us all merge as one. BUT now is the time, my children, for us all, for you all to re-unite, re-unite into oneness, into one being, one aspect of the multi-dimensional you. You need to understand you are the all, the all is you. It is the oneness of life that each and every one of you, are looking to and will experience.

Oneness is something that you will find a hard concept to feel and experience, as it has been a long time since any of you have experienced it in this time, in this way and most of all WITH CONCIOUSNESS, making you feel more alive, more alert and yet with a sense of calming and knowing you cannot even imagine.

There is no longer a thought; thought will simply be a vessel, a tool, much like a cup holds water, to be used for its purpose of consciousness and connectivity to your human vessel.

It is time to understand: the cells of your human vessel exist in multi-dimensional transvergence of layers within multi-realms of reality. It is simply not three-dimensional, as is your most frequent level of consciousness. By being more conscious of these layers of existence, it links all these layers of existence into a conscious living reality.

We cannot explain or even begin to describe in your limited language of words what the level of reality really is.

It is infinite, it is indescribable and we need to introduce these things slowly, otherwise it will blow your mind and this is not our desire. So the sounds, colours, feelings you each experience are your fanfare of desire, your own fanfare of timelessness and gradually, as each one of you acclimatise to these new frequencies of awareness, so we will introduce deeper levels of being. But dear ones, do not fear, for it is magnificent indeed and there is SO MUCH MORE to come.

You will come to know the meaning of Alchemy, the true meaning of multi-dimensional existence, in this lifetime, in this now.

So we embrace you in and with love.

Anshallah, ansitu, Codoli.

Illumination

So be still, my children of the light, for it is within and without you must go. Use the rainbow of enlightenment to enhance your vibration.

Each level, each layer of your being is blossoming into beautiful flowers of illumination, it is for you to decide what it is you wish to be. Create a garden of beauty, divinement and wonderment.

Each one of your unique beings of existence will be activated – multi-layers of existence and vibration. Choose to experience these, choose to create your garden, your garden of beauty. It is for you to know, to experience, to manifest that which your heart and soul desires. So hear your heart, my children, we are connecting to you through the myriads of the star systems. Listen to these energies, my dear ones, when you have a moment, listen to those sounds not normally heard, see those particles you do not normally see, feel those vibrations of emotions you do not normally feel. For when you take notice of this in your human body, your human vessel, this will allow those energies to integrate consciously into your being. This raising of your consciousness or vibration is the magnificent path of illumination and ascension. For understand, my children, that ascension is the path to complete love, complete joy and complete freedom.

So now let's speak of colours. For every colour of the rainbow has a unique vibration and each colour within the colour, each hue has a unique vibration of illumination.

Use the colours that have been given, notice them as they naturally occur in nature and then you will come to know that which is already known, which is how a colour will assist you in your process of evolution.

When you use colour in your adornment, your food, in your machines — choose the colour and know how this may help you.

Understand how the similarities and polarities in your life are also mirrored and reflected in colours. In colours as separate vibrations, to the wonderful evolving essence of energy, that makes up each and every one of you.

Balance

Balance is about transmission, transmission is about balance, balance of thy self, balance of those around you. Balance inside and out, balance of thoughts, words and deeds. When you are in balance, dear ones, all is well, all is calm, all is still.

The collective consciousness of all that is, remains as is. Balance is the yin and the yang, the masculine and the feminine, two polarities appearing as opposites, but just being different, contradicting and yet identical parts of the whole.

You are unique individuals, unique aspects of the divine and as such, each and every one of you will need differing things to keep in balance. They are different aspects of the same elements. The same elements will work with you all.

They are basic aspects of the soul connected and entrusted in the human vessel. So they are the aspects that bring you joy, being and being in and with nature, connecting with your soul, walking, movement, music, fun, frivolity, all emotions and energies that will calm, balance and uplift.

Your whole entity comprises of many physical and non-physical aspects, the many auric fields or layers or what others might call energy centres or bodies like the emotional body.

It does not matter what you perceive or believe, but whatever it is that you believe all these aspects of yourself need to be in balance. The brain, the ego, the chakras, the emotions, all in balance.

There are many tools that we have provided you with that can help. Some of these are based on words such as books, cards and poems. These are vibrations of sight and thought. Others are more visual vibrations such as pictures, films, colours.

Sound has a different vibration; sound is very powerful, very cleansing and immediate. Sound affects all physical cells, all physical reality simultaneously without aspects or activation of physical thought.

Remember, my children, not all vibrations are helpful to all of you all of the time. So listen to your body, listen to how it feels and when all is in alignment, when you feel love then these sounds, words, actions and pictures are the best ones for you at this time.

12.12.12 (12:12)

❋

The following text was given to me after I asked for some information about 12.12.12. for a gathering I was holding to celebrate this grand day.

❋

Dear Ones, so you have come together today, at this point, at this time, so all the energies of the earth can merge as one, so you can be part of this merging, part of this emergence into one full pulsating heart of life.

Join now with all your fellow beings of light, those conscious, those less so, for it is the acceptance of your oneness, that true beauty, true and pure love is able to emerge. This day, this time, like a few before and a few to come, holds great power in creation and embodiment of the one: the one Soul, the one Mother Father God, the one Earth Gaia in all the individual and collective glories.

Let your heart open to the experience of creation, let your heart open to abundant and unconditional love, and all the lifetimes you have had before and yet to come, should you so choose, be merged with all the great beings of lights: the Eloheim, Sanader, Jesus and the Christ energy, Archangel Michael, Archangel Uriel, Archangel Raphael, Archangel Oriel, Buddha, Krishna, Mohammed, the Galactic Council of Elders, all the Fairies, all the Elves, Salamanders, the Protectors of the Earth, the Dolphins, the Unicorns, the Ascended Masters, St Germaine, the Arcturians, the Sirians, and all the Multi-Dimensional Beings from the Multi-Verses across the Cosmos and finally beautiful Mother Earth, Gaia, who has sacrificed herself to allow multiple cleansing of not only the people of the Earth, but across the whole of Creation.

Now feel this energy and bring this into your living vessel of a supra-being of light, a physical manifestation of God. Allow this inter connectedness to fill and permeate every cell, every atom of your being, so you embody all that is. And use this light within you, to go out into the world, out into the Cosmos, to transform every person you meet, every particle of energy you become conscious of, and fill with light.

And so as you embody this oneness with all of creation, feel the true essence of unconditional love, for this is who you are, always have been and always will be.

We love you unconditionally, call upon this time (when you so wish) to continue be filled with love, with light. Go forth on your path, serenely, magnificently and humbly.

We leave you, in Peace, as Peace, in Love, as Love, Anstillah, Ansti, Codolli.

What's in a Dream?

❖

I was having a lot of very "interesting dreams" and I asked what all this dreaming and remembering was all about for me. I was given this poem.

❖

What's in a dream, no one can know

Maybe the chance to experience, the chance to grow

For in your dreams things can be done and said

That could only be in your head

For if in reality these things were acted out or came true

The gravity and magnitude to behold may be too great

For the simply human soul to chew

So go with your dreams with all your might

And worry not if you wake up in a fright

It is simply a growth of the human soul

With no necessity for attachment or worry

No necessity for an outcome

Just to feel and know that your soul is growing

Always

Worlds Collide

❂

I was given this poem after an incident happened outside an army barracks, when a local off-duty soldier was killed in broad daylight, in what appeared to be a religiously motivated killing.

❂

When two worlds collide

All grieve from the inside

Deep hatred, excitement, compassion and love

Opposites apart, yet together, below and above

Black and white, day and night

Hatred and love

Never apart

Machetes, knives and a gun

Acted out in the daylight, in the sun

Blood, cuts, galore

Morbid onlookers gawping at the gore

What we ask is the point of all this?

To help humanity, come to a point of bliss

The Blossom

It was spring and the blossom was out everywhere. (I am fortunate to be surrounded by blossom trees and live in a blossom tree lined street.) This little ditty came to me.

A Blossom is a blossom

Red, white, pink in every hue

A fragrance so alluring

It attracts all living bees

So encapsulating your being

It brings you to your knees

The dawn breaks

The wind shakes

The blossom is no more

It has fallen to the floor

A carpet galore

Cleo

❁

Cleo is one my cats that I have had the pleasure of living with
for fifteen years. Her sister sadly passed away a few years ago
and she has now reached the grand old age of seventeen.

❁

Slow and serene

The movement of age

Grace and serenity

Never an obscenity

Well maybe one

When provoked by the young

A lady of beauty

A Goddess to behold

A gentle soul

One from a mould

A compassion so deep

You can only weep

Never to escape my heart

Even if we ever part

Can I Choose to Feel Love?

❀

This poem came to me after I was contemplating my navel about a relationship.

❀

Can I choose to feel love and who may that be?

The postman, the teacher or just me?

I may feel love in any form I choose,

It does not judge, it is not my muse

Love is a gift, a vibration, a feeling

To open your heart to giving and receiving

To place another connected to your heart

Whether you are together or apart

Love is in what you say and what you do

To each and every being, should you so choose

So think not that love is just for a special someone

It's for family, friends and indeed all living ones

There is no further explanation required

Just simply to love all as you are inspired

Letting Go

✿

This poem came to me after I was contemplating letting go of a relationship.

✿

Letting go is simply so

For it implies that whatever it is

Was yours to have, to hold

But attachment is simply a state of being

A state of satisfaction

A state of inner worship on something external

Think not of losing that which is most dear

Feel it as a passing of a sacred beloved

Worship onto another

Allowing more room in your heart

To worship and adore your own love

Your own imbuement to external

and eternal multi-dimensional love

With all, for all, as one

The Dance of Life

❧

I was waiting to join in with a dance lesson of Ceroc (a mixture between Salsa and Jive) and this little poem came to me – it makes me smile.

❧

One step, two step three and more

Turn and swizzle and out the door

Play the music, fast and slow

Round and round with nowhere to go

Flat heels, high heels, dance pumps

All sorts of attire

Jeans, skirts, trousers and a dress

Some looking gorgeous, some casual, some a bit of a mess

Come together in a collective night of dance

Some mesmerised, some nonchalant, some as if in a trance

Bodies moving, feet tapping

Almost like a happy clapping

Sexual undertones emanating from a few

Subtly touching acting as if being true

So all this in one night of dance

What more could you want given half a chance

To Move or Not to Move ... that is the question.

Oh to Be Great

❁

*Often I sit and wonder what it would be like to be
and to feel like one of the great ones and how I can
endeavour to be like this, to embody this. This came
to me.*

❁

Oh to be great

Like Jesus, Buddha, Mohamed, Krishna and all

But know your magnificence, hear our call

A creation of God or whatever you choose to feel

No lesser being

Than any great ones that come to your mind

All flesh and feelings, all the same kind

If only you could know how great you all are

Your uniqueness, your oneness

If you feel near or far

For at our source we are beings of love

Greatness is who we are

Buddha was not Buddha without a human soul

Jesus would not have had a place to go

Nor Mohammed a journey to sow

Krishna a living breathing embodiment of love

None of this possible without the greatness from above

Above and below, nowhere to go

All part of the greatness of the collective human soul

The Meeting

When I met you there was stillness

When I tasted you there was madness

When I touched you there was illness

When I soothed you there was wellness

When we came together there was oneness

True Beauty

True beauty is when lips meet for the first time

True beauty is not caring if the sun doth shine

True beauty is when worlds collide

True beauty is honesty from the soul

True beauty is seeing for eternity

And not minding it does not end

True beauty is seeing your own reflection in the lake

And loving what you see

True beauty is not finding any answers

True beauty is seeing the silence in the snow

True beauty is feeling another's breath on your skin

True beauty is sitting, watching, listening and feeling

Troubled Waters

❄

This came to me after I met someone new and felt the depth and trouble of the human aspect of their soul.

❄

They say still waters run deep, but all waters may run deep

For at their surface, at their source

They may be a mere trickle or indeed a deep pool

It matters not, for eventually the trickle will become a pool

Or the pool will become a trickle

But in the water there is still depth

Still hidden yet clearly visible matter of everything

And yet nothingness together

See through the windows of visible clarity

Yet perceive only that which is within your reach

Within your sight of understanding

But know this even within troubled water

There is a stillness to be found

A stillness to be felt

A stillness to be grown

For in the ripple of stillness

The troubles of water are calmed

And brought back to peace again

Back to love again

Back to the stillness of the moment of now

Who Are You?

Who are you that makes me sing?

With a vibration in my heart as if in the presence of a king

Who are you that makes me smile?

All sadness and pain dissolve even just for a while

Who are you with such a gentle caressing touch

That make me feel oh so much

Who are you that I see?

Maybe a reflection of me

Maybe the soul of humanity

Or maybe just how it is meant to be

Nature

See Nature

Feel Nature

Love Nature

Be Nature

What is Love?

Love is a wondrous and curious thing

It can come anytime not just in spring

It opens up a door, like never before

A mountain top view, with nothing askew

A sunrise, A sunset

Orange glowing shimmering sighs

As the sun and moon collide

Deep russets of autumn,

A cool mountainous glow of the moon

Half open, half closed but only till dawn

The shrills of the chorus, an enlightening sound

Our ears and body vibrate

With the tone of something newfound

Of wondrous beauty to rise once again

As another dawn breaks for all of eternity. Amen

Times Gone By

❁

*I am lucky enough to visit Norway both in a work
capacity and for pleasure several times a year and I
have a deep connection with the land and the people.
Whilst going through my usual feeling of grief,
waiting at the airport to depart, I imagined the
mountains, looked at the Fjords and this story came
to me of times before.*

❁

The hills are calling

The water and fjords drawing

The yearn of my heart

To be still to be embraced by the land

Ancient times gone by

An array of stars in the sky

Night fall beacons

The crest of the moon alights all around

The thickness of the forest surrounds

Eyes shimmering with a hypnotic glow

Shadows moving with nowhere to go

A trickle as the stream approaches exploring the earth

The trees creak far above the land

A flicker of light, a slice through the air

Another fallen bear

The sounds of the forest, never to return, never to escape

All is still, yet death hangs in the air

Man or beast, beast or man

Why do we ravage the peace in this land

The Meaning of Who You Are -

A Human Being

When the energies between time and space

Evolve and dissolve

Only the infinite is possible, only the infinite exists

There is no need for anything more

You are all dear children of God

Everything, yet nothing, at the same time

All exists as never before

Do not limit yourselves my dear children

To that which you know

That which you understand

For this is limiting your existence of the now

And we say again: you are infinite

So understand this in every aspect of your being

The word being is the nearest word

In your human language

That only starts to describe

The essence of who and what you are

Leaning to emulate

Learning to experience

Learning to remember

Learning how to evolve

Understand again we will tell you until you understand

In the essence of your being

You are magnificent, you are infinite

We are infinite, infinite indeed

Open up to dream

Dream and live your possibilities and your impossibilities

For in your impossibilities you will find more of yourselves

More of who you truly are

And as you discover who you are

So you will discover even more of who you are

And this you will then understand

What the meaning of being is

Jasmina

✦

Jasmina is one my cats that I have had the pleasure of living with for four years. I was told by several friends (who are quite psychic) that I would have a kitten that was female, black and white and had the presence of a princess. She is all these things and more.

✦

An alluring purr

Soft fur

The twitch of a tail

A gentle meow

A head butt

A kiss on the chin

Run up the stairs in a spin

A crunch in the mouth

A crunch in the feet

A dog never wanting to meet

No noise or loud din

Never eating from a tin

Eyes half closed

Sitting on a chair

How could she never be there?

How Do I Know You're Special?

For all those special people that are, have been and are yet to appear in my life

When I look in your eyes and feel the depth of your soul

When I touch your heart and feel it glow

When I know what you're thinking, words on my lips in synchronisation ready for speaking

When your smile radiates all the stars in the sky

When your words soothe all that goes by

When the clouds pass, with the dew on the grass

Not a care for each, as the days go by

When I just catch your eye

The world changes in that moment

That's when I know you're special

A Room's View

❀

Whilst spending a number of days at a beautiful retreat/spa, where I had needed time for rest and recuperation, I was looking out of the window and felt this poem.

❀

The silent drops of rain fall

The grass slightly shimmering from the view

The trees deathly still

Rebirth hangs in the air

As if like a silent prayer

The sky try's to alight through the cloudy haze so bright

The shrills in the air infrequent and so tight

The sight clear yet somehow a mist fills the air

Not a sound lingers

Even as the bushes tremble so slightly

The moon awakes, the dawn breaks

All is calm serene and still

Another rebirth, another hill

Ever changing, ever the same

Never to return to this moment of pain

To this moment of bliss

When darkness and light

Fall into the abyss

A Witches Tale

A wonderful being I have the pleasure of knowing inspired me to write this poem for her.

Such a magnificent witch to behold

So potent is her magic she need not be told

They get together and they brew and they stew

What else are they to do?

Fear not, for it is not a pot of evil grot they invoke

It is love, enlightenment and justice

So's to provoke

They come together in their clans so enlightening

But do not worry, you will never catch them fighting

So if this witch should pass you by

Do not sigh, let out a large cry

So you catch her eye

And then you will never regret a day gone by

✺

'It is important to work on your art regularly,

because that takes you to a place

which is your very own vibration.'

(Viktória Gy Duda)

✺

A Warrior's Day

✿

Another inspirational poem that came to me while at the airport in Norway, taking me back to another life, as a Viking.

✿

The days are harsh, the nights are long

Daylight brings a sorrowful song

Another battle, bodies askew

The night was long, the fight overdue

The sounds of the battle ringing in the land

The red flowing waters and scarlet coloured sand

The cries of the battle now a mere whimpering sound

Of the last dying warriors spewed across the land

The excitement of the battle fuelling the gore

A way of life for which there is no cure

A glimpse of devotion

A glimpse of salvation

The terror, the hatred, cruelty and brutality awash

Yet no way out of this monstrous mash

The one way to end, to escape this madness

I extinguish my life and I end this sadness

At last I am free, to feel the beauty of the night

At last I am free, to no longer feel fright

The next journey I take will

Be one of serenity love and peace

To help end this madness and

For the wheels of karma to cease

A Moment in Time

❁

When I pondered one day about "Life the Universe and Everything" (Number 42) I realised that each moment is magical

❁

A moment in time when the sun does not shine

A moment in time when the white blanket of snow

Covers all that may grow

A moment in time at the dawn of spring

When snowdrops open their hearts and the daffodils sing

A moment in time when the wind bites your face

A moment in time when all is in haste

A moment in time you are drowning in pain

A moment in time when nothing will ever be the same

A moment in time when the earth meets the sky

A moment in time as life passes you by

A moment in time when darkness is all around

A moment in time when you cannot be found

A moment in time when the sky lights your soul

A moment in time when there is little to know

A moment in time when all is completed

A moment in time when all is depleted

A moment in time is all we have

A moment in time that lasts for eternity

❋

'A perfect synergy of spirit and humanness (humanity)

coming together in perfect embodiment'

(Sue Barker, when reading a poem)

❋

Look at Love

Look at love and see what's there

It has nothing to do with colour of hair

It has nothing to do with a face so fair

A body so taught it manifests a curious thought

Love is in a smile to behold

A heart overflowing as if a chest of gold

A presence of being

With a mind still seeing

A caress of a touch, no words could say that much

A stillness, a knowing, eyes overflowing

Shining brightly into the world

Shows a statement of love, gifted from above

A kind word, a kind deed, without thought or heed

A generous soul, everyone wants to know

A smile from an angel's heart

A presence you do not want to part

Look at love, are these all a display

Of who and what you portray

Collective Consciousness

❂

When I was with a good friend in Norway, she had invited a number of her friends over for a night in. Whilst sitting and listening (as I cannot speak Norwegian), I picked up the kinetic energy between the group, it was fabulous. And this was what was explained to me about people coming together in their groups or gatherings.

❂

So when you come together in your groups

The untied cells merge into oneness

This oneness is who you are

So feel and experience the breath of life

Listen to your heart

Feel with your breath

Experience with your being

Be in your stillness

Be in the collective stillness and

You will find your connection is exponential

The expansion of the universe becomes you

Is incorporated into your unique oneness

As a conscious collectiveness

Choose to link to these collective vibrations and

They will envelope your being more and more

Into the now

You become the now and the now becomes you

What's in a Decision?

A new road, a new pathway

A clear road ahead to imagine and create your dreams

A worn out dirt track with many bends and snarls

Brambles, tearing at your skin

Never to awaken from the pattern of repetition

Perhaps the road is both of these

A nightmare and a dream all rolled into one

Whatever the decision, it is always a choice

To choose a dream or a nightmare or worse:

The two together

So when a decision needs to be made

Tread lightly, tread carefully

And most of all tread slowly

Then any decision you can be sure is one of your choosing

Where Do We Go from Here?

Where do we go from here in this place of fear

For tightness and contortion in my body I feel

My mind a whirling mass of clogs and wheels

My emotions ravaged to the very core

My soul hidden beneath the floor

Chaos and confusion reigns supreme

As fear obliterates my dream

One step at a time for each atom of fear

One step at a time and slowly the love will appear

One step at a time

Loneliness

❀

I went through a time when I felt very lonely (in a relationship!) and this came to me.

❀

The dark nights, the cold frights

The yearning for love, never a moment away

Stomach churns, the brain fogs

The bones moan, somehow without a groan

The empty vessel, the hollow sight

Deep into the night

An illusion of the mind

If only to find

The loneliness inside, does not need to hide

For it is not real

You just need to feel...

The wind in your hair

The smell of the air

The luscious mountain brook

The trees that crook

The flowers in bloom

The butterflies loom

A dawn breaking sky

The heron as it may fly

Another soul's smile

Just take a while

Loneliness can then not be found

It has run aground

Judgement Day

❋

I had been thinking about a situation and felt I was being very judgemental – this advice popped into my head.

❋

When judgements come, let them stay

So you can acknowledge their presence

Any time of night or day

For in that moment when awareness comes

Choose which way, your consciousness will sway

Let heaven come to your door and

Guide those judgements away

For a judgement of another

Is only a judgement of yourself

Disguised in a belief it may bring you

Wealth, or abundance, or superiority, or health

None of this is true for judgements

In effect can only make you blue

So when you know a judgement has arisen

In a thought, a word, a deed

Take heed

For on this day

Take a moment to pray and

Dissolve that judgement into love and away

Otherwise it may turn out to be your judgement day

Soul to Soul

When souls meet

It touches down to your feet

It sweeps you away

Forever and a day

A soul is true and pure

But the human vessel may be living in a sewer

like manure

So although the souls can be oh so joyful when they meet

and touch

The human vessel may struggle to combine as beautifully

as much

It is just how it is meant to be

So humans through their soul can learn to see

Heart Awakening

❦

I had been having a feeling that things were coming more alive for me...

❦

As your heart awakens

Your senses expand to fill the void

That was never known before your heart had grown

Your eyes seeing the stillness, the movement

The dance of life

Your nose filled with colours and aromas and

Tastes of the day and night

The touch of the lily and the mighty oak

A sense so pure you could almost choke

The feelings inside imbued from another

From nature, of love

So innocent, so knowing

So connected to all and above

The trickle of water zinging in your mouth,

A coolness, a clearness so profound

You never tasted before

The vibrations of sound, so near so far

Alighting your ears to drink from its core

No visible sound can be heard as the leaves move

Yet somehow the gentle rustle is nestled in your being

And so the heart awakens...

An Epiphany

Can be simple, can be small

Cannot seem to matter at all

But in the moment when awareness comes

The whole world can change

Just by the movement of drums

Just by the change of a thought

Just by the words that are brought

A road, a new path, a new door

Opens up a new eternity never dreamed of before

A simple gesture, from one to another

Can harness the strength of love from sister to brother

So never wonder what the gesture can hold

For an epiphany can come forth without being told